THE BIG BOOK OF
NATURE

PAUL STERRY

GALLERY BOOKS
An Imprint of W. H. Smith Publishers Inc.
112 Madison Avenue
New York City 10016

First published in the United States in 1990 by Gallery Books,
an imprint of W.H. Smith Publishers. Inc.,
112 Madison Avenue, New York, New York 10016

By arrangement with The Octopus Publishing Group Limited,
Michelin House, 81 Fulham Road, London SW3 6RB

ISBN 0-8317-0864-6

Printed in Great Britain by BPCC Paulton Books Ltd

Gallery Books are available for bulk purchase for sales promotions and
premium use. For details write or telephone the Manager of Special
Sales, W.H. Smith Publishers, Inc., 112 Madison Avenue, New York,
New York 10016. (212) 532-6600

CONTENTS

WHAT IS NATURE?

The study of nature is the study of living things. Both plants and animals are living: they grow, feed, and reproduce, and give rise to new generations of plants and animals which ensure the survival of the species. With advanced forms of life, it is usually easy to tell the difference between a plant and an animal but with more primitive species it can be quite difficult.

Wherever we look around us we see examples of nature. Immense trees, fields of grasses, colorful flowers, ferns, and mosses from the plant kingdom, and worms, snails, butterflies, frogs, birds, mammals, and many other creatures from the animal kingdom.

The plants and animals that can be found almost everywhere in the world around us are part of what is called the natural environment. Many of the things in this natural environment are not living at all, such as rocks, rivers, clouds, rain, and snow. But all of these things are essential for life to survive.

The plants and animals we see today are all descended from simple forms of life and over millions of years they have adapted to the changing environment. This process is called evolution.

Scientists have devised a system, known as classification, that divides living things into groups, such as mammals, birds, reptiles, ferns, mosses, etc. Members of each group are recognized by features they have in common. In this book we will study each group, and learn about some of the mysteries of the natural world.

Right: Classification of the animal kingdom.

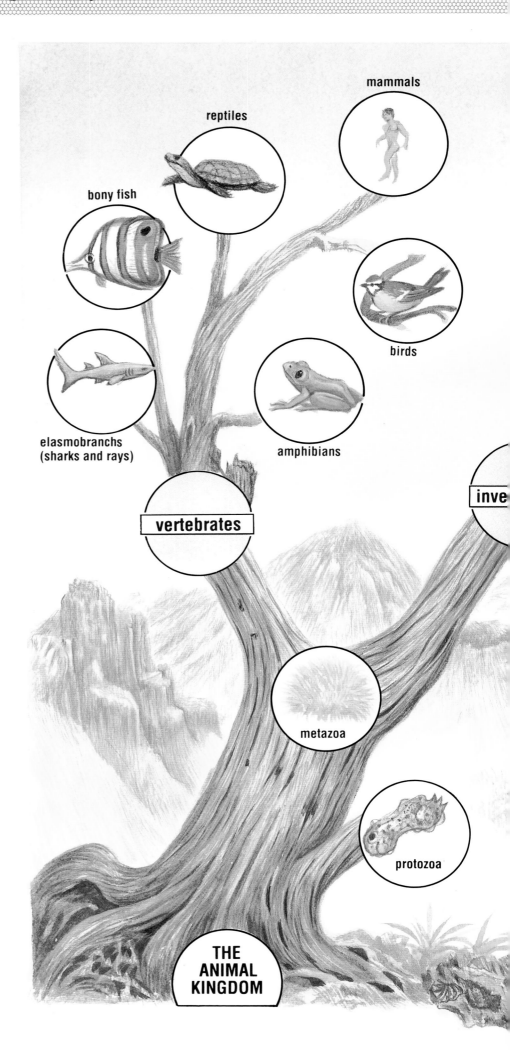

mammals

reptiles

bony fish

birds

elasmobranchs
(sharks and rays)

amphibians

vertebrates

inve

metazoa

protozoa

THE
ANIMAL
KINGDOM

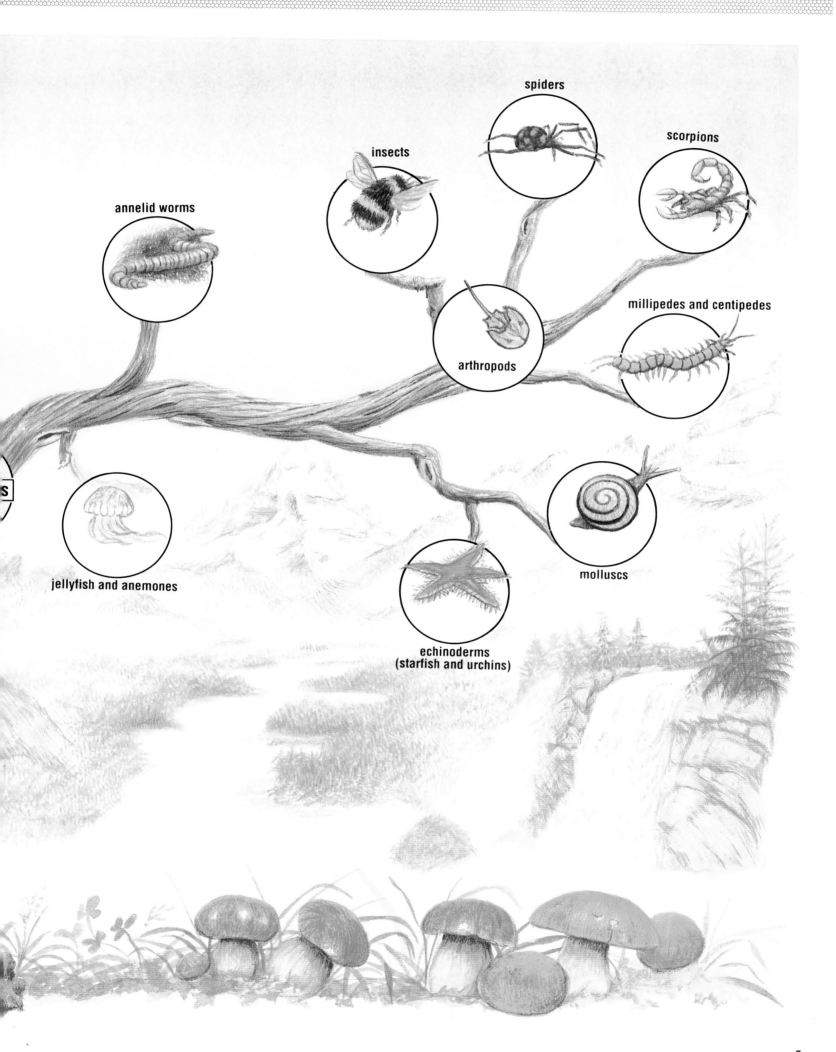

spiders

insects

scorpions

annelid worms

arthropods

millipedes and centipedes

jellyfish and anemones

molluscs

echinoderms
(starfish and urchins)

MICROSCOPIC LIFE

The world around us is full of plants and animals easily seen with our own eyes. However, there are also vast numbers of microscopic creatures. They are so small that thousands can be found in a single drop of pond water or sea water and they cannot be seen without the aid of a microscope to magnify them. A microscope is made up of a series of glass lenses contained in a tube. When you look through the lenses, microscopic plants and animals become enlarged so that you can see them clearly.

Bacteria are among the smallest of these tiny creatures. They are everywhere around us – in the air, in the water, and in our food. Most do not do us any harm but a few are dangerous and can cause illnesses. Others are important because they cause decay and make things rot. When bacteria attack dead matter, such as the fall leaves that drop to the ground, they allow nutrients to return to the soil.

Right: Although they are both microscopic plants, spirogyra are multi-celled, and diatoms consist of only one cell. An amoeba is a protozoan – a single-celled animal. Protozoans form the basis of all underwater food chains.

diatom

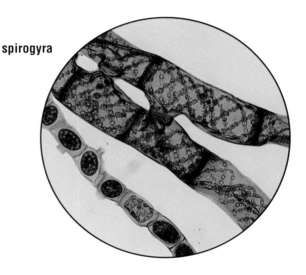
spirogyra

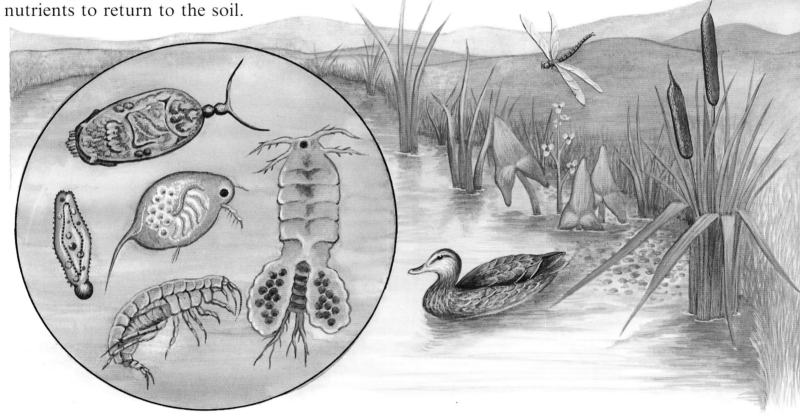

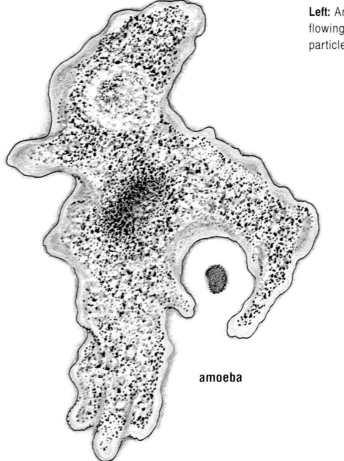

Left: An amoeba feeds by flowing round a food particle and trapping it.

amoeba

All living things are made up of cells, but many of the smallest animals are so tiny they consist of only one cell. These are called protozoans, and they often live in water. Algae and diatoms are also made of only one cell and often look similar to protozoa but they are, in fact, plants, not animals. Algae can often be seen as a green covering on the surface of ponds.

The young stages of common seashore creatures such as starfishes and crabs are also very small. Together, all these microscopic plants and animals that are found floating in water are called plankton. During warm weather, plankton can become so abundant that it makes the water go cloudy.

Below: Microscopic animals, shown here greatly magnified, are found in both fresh water and sea water, and in a variety of shapes.

7

SOFT-BODIED ANIMALS

Right: This colorful clownfish lives in tropical seas. It is quite at home among the tentacles of this sea anemone. The anemone's tentacles are covered in poisonous stinging cells which are used to catch its food. The clownfish is immune to the stings, however, and so is protected from its enemies. Several smaller kinds of anemone are found on rocky shores around Europe.

Right: This strange worm is called an amphitrite. It lives in estuaries around the coasts of Britain and Europe. The worm has a soft body which is divided into segments. It lives buried in the mud. In order to feed, it sends out tentacles across the surface of the mud and drags back particles of food. The red gills help the animal to breathe.

Left: The oceans around the world are full of soft-bodied animals called jellyfish. These are a few of the types that can be found. If they are washed onto the shore they look just like jelly. Some jellyfish only float with the current but others can swim quite well. Their long tentacles catch fish and other small marine animals. These are then transferred to the mouth, on the underside of the body, and eaten.

Many animals have neither bones nor hard shells so their bodies are soft, like the familiar earthworm. The earthworm's body is made up of many segments, each with its own muscles, and by contracting these the worm can move. Bristles on the sides of the worm help it grip the surface of the soil. For protection, it burrows into the ground.

Many types of worms are found on the seashore. The lugworm lives in a U-shaped burrow in the mud. In order to feed, it swallows mud and filters out any food. Whatever is left is passed out from the body and left on the shore as small heaps of mud or casts. Other species have tentacles to catch particles of food and drag them back to their burrow.

Leeches are flat worms which live in fresh-water. To feed, they have suckers with which they suck fluids from other animals. Tapeworms and nematode worms are parasites. They live inside other animals and absorb liquid food from their host's intestines.

Jellyfish live in the open oceans. They swim near the surface of the water and have long tentacles with stinging cells to catch fish and other animals. Sea anemones also have stinging tentacles but live attached to rocks. In some tropical species, clownfish live among the tentacles and help keep the anemone clean. They don't get harmed by the sting because they are immune to the poison.

Corals live in tropical seas, in large colonies known as coral reefs. Each animal is like a small anemone but they make a hard case around their bodies.

SLUGS AND SNAILS

Some animals protect their soft bodies with a shell, for example the snail, and these all belong to a group called molluscs. Mollusc shells come in all shapes and sizes. Some are spiral, some have colorful markings, while others have shells divided into two halves. Walk along the seashore and you will soon see the variety of forms.

Some molluscs are very large. The African land snail is as big as a fist and its body is too large to be withdrawn into the shell. Some clams found in the sea are large enough to trap a man's foot.

Limpets live on the seashore and have a conical shell which protects them from the battering waves. Clams, mussels, and oysters have shells divided into two halves and are called bivalves. They feed by sucking in water through a tube and trapping the food inside the shell. This is called filter-feeding. The inside of the shell is often beautifully marked and has a shiny surface known as mother-of-pearl. In oysters, this shiny material is used by the animal to make pearls.

Slugs are slightly different because they have only a small shell or sometimes none at all. Like snails, they glide along on a film of sticky mucus which is produced by their "foot." Sea slugs lack shells, too. Many species of sea slug have beautiful colors and are poisonous.

Cuttlefish, squid, and octopuses or octopi are also molluscs. Many species have skin which can change color to match the surroundings. They have good eyesight and long tentacles used for catching prey such as fish and crabs.

common mussel

limpet

common piddock

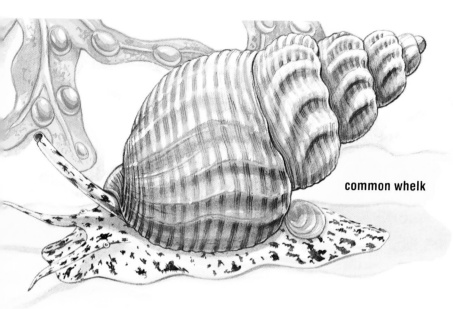

common whelk

t scallop

Right: In wet weather, tree slugs climb tree trunks to eat the lichens which grow on the bark. Unlike snails, slugs lack an external shell.

pelican's foot shell

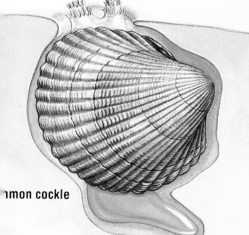

mon cockle

Right: The snail's body is coiled to fit inside the protective shell. The foot is used to help the animal move. The head has eyes, a mouth, and sensitive feelers.

THE INSIDE OF A SNAIL

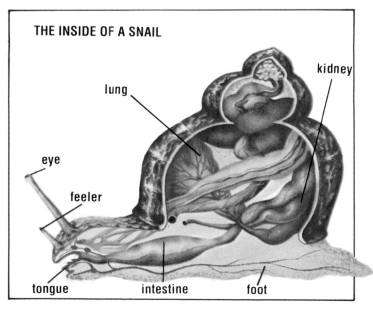

lung

kidney

eye

feeler

tongue

intestine

foot

11

INSECTS

Insects belong to the biggest group of animals on earth. There are more species of insect than of all other animals added together. They are found almost everywhere – on mountain tops, in deserts, forests, meadows – and even in fresh-water. The sea is the only place that they have not colonized.

Insects are extremely varied in appearance, from butterflies to beetles and from flies to bugs, but they all share the same characteristics. The body is divided into three main parts – the head, the thorax, and the abdomen.

The head has two eyes, mouthparts, and a pair of antennae which sense the surroundings. The thorax is the middle of the body and has two pairs of wings and three pairs of legs. The abdomen usually looks segmented and contains the digestive and reproductive systems.

Adult insects often have extremely good sight. Flies and dragonflies have particularly large eyes which are made up of hundreds of small cells. These are called compound eyes and give the insects nearly all-round vision.

Many insects are able to fly and have different types of wings. The wings of bees and dragonflies, for example, are clear, while butterflies and moths have wings covered in colorful scales. These colors may be used to camouflage the insect or to scare off predators. Some insects appear to have only one pair of wings even though they actually have two. A fly's hind pair are reduced in size, while in a beetle the front pair are hardened to protect the hind wings when at rest.

Below: Insects belong to an extremely large and varied group of animals. Flies and butterflies, for example, can fly well, while others, such as beetles, spend more time on the ground.

lacewing

gall wasp

cricket

garden tiger moth

bombardier beetle

Right: The garden tiger moth has mottled forewings. When alarmed, it spreads these to reveal orange hind wings which warn predators that it tastes unpleasant.

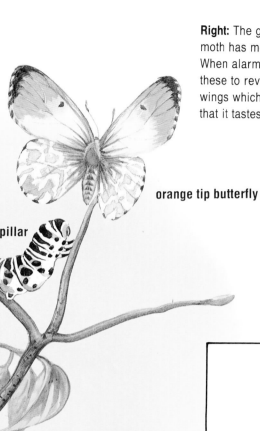

orange tip butterfly

rpillar

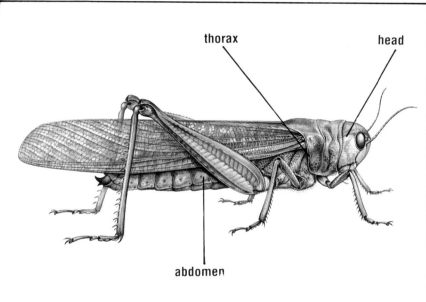

thorax   head

abdomen

Left: Like most adult insects, the locust has two pairs of wings and three pairs of legs. The body is divided into the head, the thorax, and the segmented abdomen.

bluebottle

Right: If you look carefully at the head of this fly you will see several different sense organs. Most prominent are the large eyes, called compound eyes. They are made up of lots of small lenses, and give the fly a very wide angle of vision.

INSECT LIVES

Insects go through great changes in appearance during their lives. For example, a butterfly lays eggs from which a caterpillar hatches. When fully grown, the caterpillar changes into a chrysalis and from this an adult butterfly eventually emerges. The four stages – egg, caterpillar, chrysalis, and adult – make up the life cycle of the butterfly.

The soft body of a caterpillar is protected by a tough skin. As the caterpillar grows, the skin becomes tight and from time to time it is molted. For a few hours after molting, the new skin is soft and the caterpillar can expand in size.

Grasshoppers also go through similar changes but they are more gradual. Although the young insect does not look like the adult when it hatches from the egg, in each stage of the grasshopper's life cycle it looks more and more like the adult.

lackey caterpillar

lackey

Left: Glowworm females attract males to mate with by producing a bright light from the tip of their abdomen. During the daytime glowworms live on the ground among the fallen leaves.

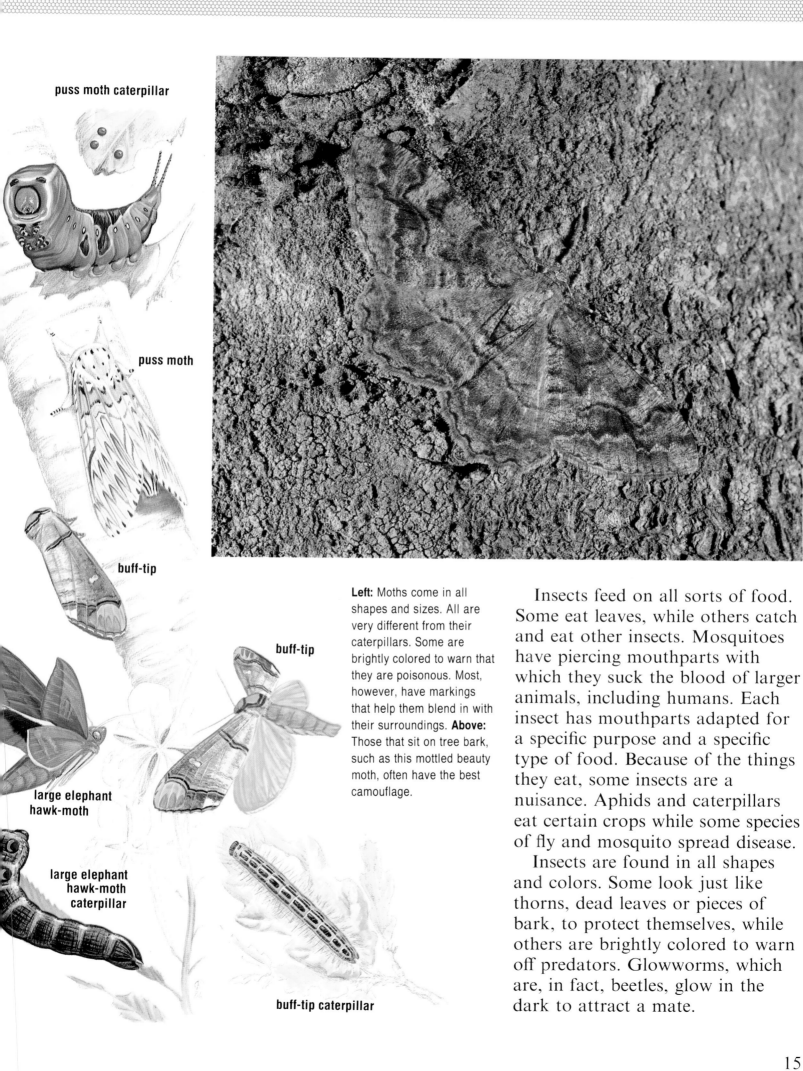

puss moth caterpillar

puss moth

buff-tip

buff-tip

large elephant
hawk-moth

large elephant
hawk-moth
caterpillar

buff-tip caterpillar

Left: Moths come in all shapes and sizes. All are very different from their caterpillars. Some are brightly colored to warn that they are poisonous. Most, however, have markings that help them blend in with their surroundings. **Above:** Those that sit on tree bark, such as this mottled beauty moth, often have the best camouflage.

Insects feed on all sorts of food. Some eat leaves, while others catch and eat other insects. Mosquitoes have piercing mouthparts with which they suck the blood of larger animals, including humans. Each insect has mouthparts adapted for a specific purpose and a specific type of food. Because of the things they eat, some insects are a nuisance. Aphids and caterpillars eat certain crops while some species of fly and mosquito spread disease.

Insects are found in all shapes and colors. Some look just like thorns, dead leaves or pieces of bark, to protect themselves, while others are brightly colored to warn off predators. Glowworms, which are, in fact, beetles, glow in the dark to attract a mate.

SPIDERS AND THEIR RELATIVES

Spiders, scorpions, millipedes, and centipedes have jointed limbs and a hardened outer skin, like the insects. They all belong to a group of animals known as arthropods. Unlike insects, however, spiders and their relatives all have four or more pairs of legs.

Spiders have four pairs of legs and a body divided into two parts. Most spiders catch their food by spinning webs of silk to trap passing insects. To make its web, a spider first makes a basic framework of silk, which looks like the spokes of a wheel, and then it spins a spiral of silk that is sticky, starting from the middle, to complete the web.

Wolf spiders do not spin webs to catch their food because they can run fast enough to catch small insects. The trap-door spider lives in tunnels in the ground, lined with silk and with a trapdoor at the entrance. When an insect comes close to the door, the spider opens the door, rushes out and catches it.

Scorpions live in hot countries around the world, both in deserts and in tropical forests. They usually spend the day hidden under stones or fallen trees. They have a pair of powerful claws at the front and a poisonous sting in the tail which is used to kill their prey.

Although centipedes and millipedes look rather similar, and both have many more legs than spiders or scorpions, there are a number of differences. Centipedes have one pair of legs on each segment and are carnivores (they eat other animals), while millipedes have two pairs of legs on each segment and eat plant matter.

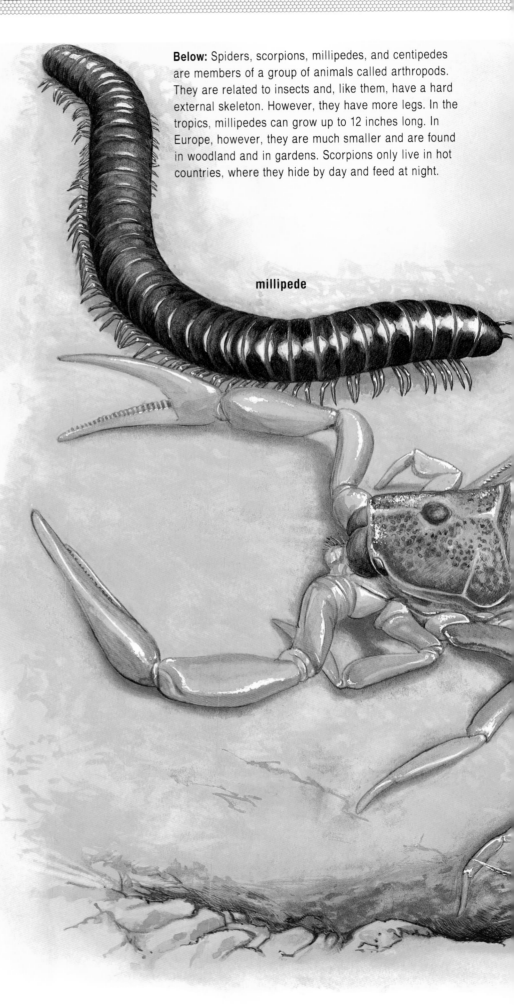

Below: Spiders, scorpions, millipedes, and centipedes are members of a group of animals called arthropods. They are related to insects and, like them, have a hard external skeleton. However, they have more legs. In the tropics, millipedes can grow up to 12 inches long. In Europe, however, they are much smaller and are found in woodland and in gardens. Scorpions only live in hot countries, where they hide by day and feed at night.

millipede

Right: Spiders come in all shapes and sizes. Biggest are the bird-eating spiders from the tropics. Garden spiders spin beautiful webs.

scorpion

centipede

bird-eating spider

wolf spider

black widow spider

garden spider

CRABS, LOBSTERS, AND SHRIMPS

Crabs, lobsters, and shrimps belong to a group of animals called crustaceans. Their bodies are made up of segments with a pair of legs on each one, but these are often hidden by a protective shell. Most crustaceans live in freshwater or in the sea, although there are some that live on land.

Crabs, lobsters, and shrimps have two pairs of antennae which can sense the water around them, and a pair of stalked eyes which can swivel. Their strong pincers hold and tear food and their mouthparts sort the particles and direct them to the mouth.

Some crabs live on the shoreline and shelter under seaweed at low tide, while others prefer deep water. Lobsters live in deep gulleys and crevices and only venture out to find food.

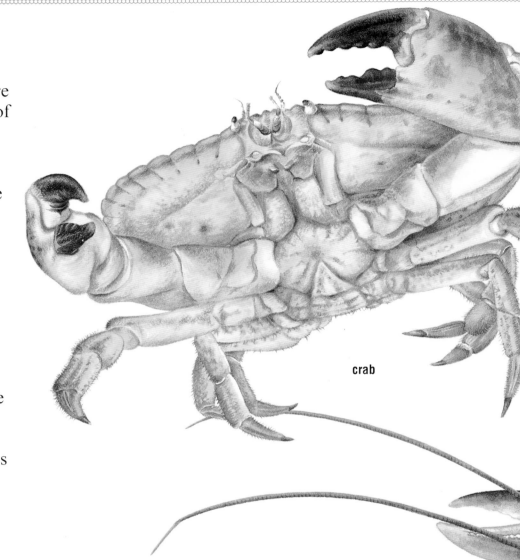

crab

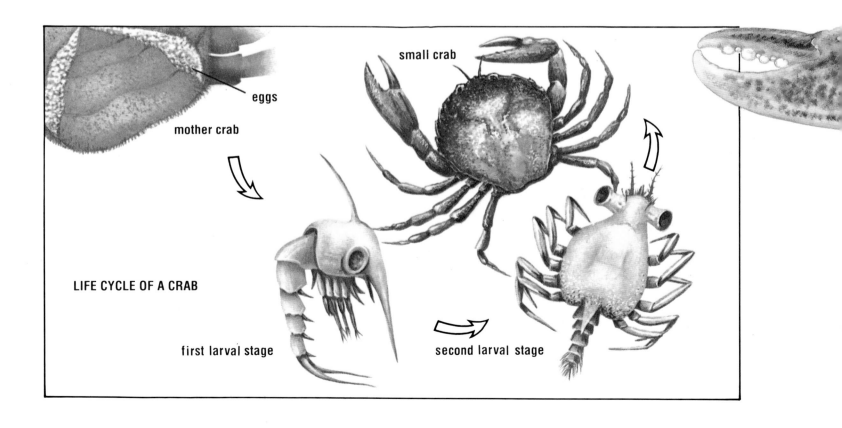

eggs

mother crab

small crab

LIFE CYCLE OF A CRAB

first larval stage

second larval stage

Because crabs have a hard outer shell they cannot grow unless they molt this from time to time. Just after shedding the shell, their body is soft and they are then called soft-shell crabs.

The young stages of crabs and lobsters are extremely small and look very different from the full-grown animals. They swim around in the open water along with other microscopic creatures. Some very numerous species of crustacean, such as water fleas and ostracods, always remain tiny.

Wood lice can be found living all over the world and, although they live on land, they are still crustaceans. Like crabs, they breathe using gills which must be kept moist at all times, so they are always found in damp places.

Above: Hermit crabs have soft bodies and live in old shells for protection. Sometimes an anemone attaches itself to the outside of the shell.

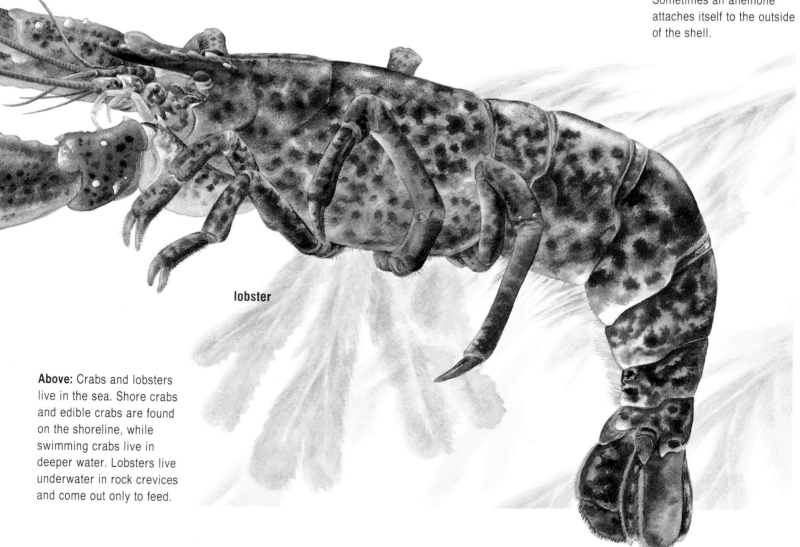

lobster

Above: Crabs and lobsters live in the sea. Shore crabs and edible crabs are found on the shoreline, while swimming crabs live in deeper water. Lobsters live underwater in rock crevices and come out only to feed.

19

ANIMALS WITH SPINY SKINS

Starfish, sea urchins, and sea cucumbers are spiny-skinned animals that live in the sea. They belong to a group of animals called echinoderms and are sometimes found in rock pools on the seashore.

Most starfish have five long arms. The upper sides of the arms are covered in tough skin and short spines, while the underside has rows of tiny tube feet. These lie on either side of grooves which all lead to the central mouth. Some starfish have short, rounded arms and are called cushion stars. Others have thin and fragile arms and are called brittle stars.

Starfish can travel along the sea bed by pumping water into their tube feet which enables the feet to move. Although they can only walk slowly, the tube feet are very strong – powerful enough to pull apart a mussel or scallop shell.

Sea urchins are covered in fearsome spines which are fixed to their hard shells. Like starfish, sea urchins have their mouths underneath their bodies. Inside the mouth are five teeth which open and close to scrape up the pieces of plant remains on which sea urchins feed. Most sea urchins are ball shaped but some are flat and are able to bury themselves in sand and mud. These urchins are known as sand dollars.

Sea cucumbers look very different from starfish and sea urchins. They have soft bodies and, although they do have spines, they are difficult to see. The mouth is at one end of the body and around the mouth are long tube feet which help the sea cucumber catch food. Sea cucumbers move slowly.

Above and left: Spiny-skinned animals, or echinoderms, live in the sea. Their bodies are protected by tough skins and spines. Sea cucumbers (**far left**) have minute spines but those of sea urchins (**left**) are very large. Sea cucumbers, sea urchins, and starfish have tube feet which help them move and feed. The tube feet of starfish (**above**) lie along the undersides of their long arms, as shown on this close-up of a crown of thorns starfish.

FISH

Fish are found in seas, rivers, and lakes throughout the world. There are probably about 20,000 different species of fish ranging from tiny fresh-water kinds, less than half an inch long, to giant whale sharks over 40 feet long. In most fish the body is covered in scales and they breathe using gills. A few can survive in air but most cannot live out of water.

Fish are perfectly suited to a life in water. Those that can swim fast are streamlined in shape, that is, the head is pointed and the body is broad, narrowing toward the tail. The tail provides the power for movement and the fins give control. As the fish swims, water goes into the mouth and out again through a covered slit on the side of the head. In this slit lie the gills which take the oxygen the fish need to survive out of the water.

Below: Fish are found everywhere, from small ponds to the depths of the oceans. Some are streamlined, like the shark, and can swim very fast. Others, such as catfish, swim at a slower pace. Piranhas have fearsome teeth with which they can tear their prey. Sea horses live among seaweeds in warm waters. They are unusual because the males look after the young fish, in a pouch in their belly.

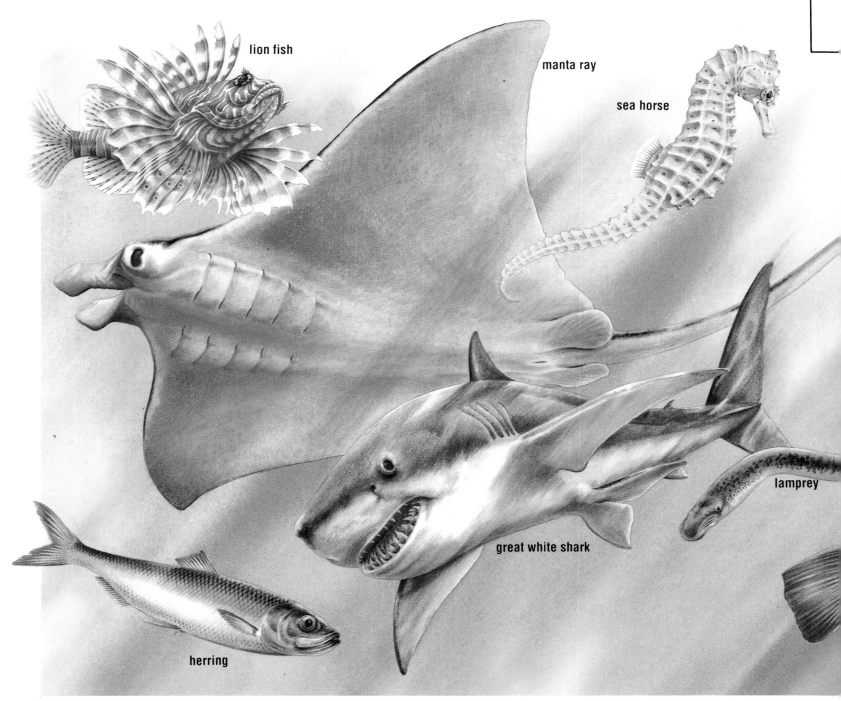

lion fish

manta ray

sea horse

lamprey

great white shark

herring

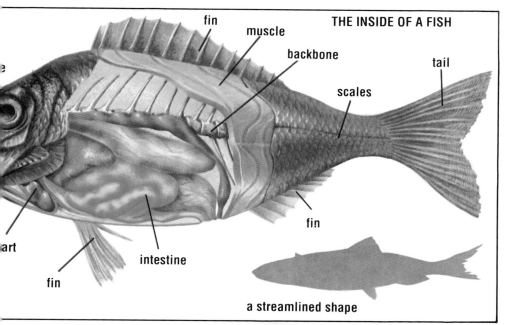

THE INSIDE OF A FISH

fin
muscle
backbone
tail
scales
fin
intestine
fin
a streamlined shape

Fish that live on the bottom of seas and lakes are often a different shape from those which are active swimmers. Eels are long and thin, while brill and flounder have flattened bodies. Adult flatfish have both eyes on the upper side of their body. In young fish, they are on opposite sides but they move as the fish grows and changes shape.

Inside the bodies of most fish there is a swim bladder full of air, which makes the fish buoyant. Sharks do not have a swim bladder and therefore have to swim all the time to avoid sinking.

Some fish can even "fly". Flying fish leap out of the water and glide through the air with the help of large fins.

Above: Fish swim using their fins. Power comes from the tail, while the other fins control the direction.

bream

piranha

perch

catfish

AMPHIBIANS

Frogs, toads, newts, and salamanders can survive on land but have to return to water to breed. They are descended from creatures that first ventured onto land 300 million years ago. Although there are lots of amphibians still alive today, there are not as many kinds now and they tend to be much smaller.

Frogs are common in lakes and ponds in most countries. Each spring they lay masses of jelly-covered eggs under the water. These are known as frog spawn. The young frogs that hatch out are quite unlike adult frogs and are called tadpoles. They breathe by using gills and feed on pond plants. Their back legs soon appear and a little later their front legs start to grow. They then begin to feed on pond animals and their tails gradually shrink. Eventually they look like little frogs, about half an inch long. At the same time, they begin to breathe with lungs and can then leave the water.

Toads also congregate in ponds in spring but they usually lay their eggs in long strings rather than in masses. Certain toads and frogs have loud songs and calls for attracting mates. The biggest frog is the goliath frog which lives in Africa. It can grow to about 10 inches in length.

Newts and salamanders are also amphibians but unlike frogs and toads they have tails. Most are fairly small, although the Japanese giant salamander grows up to 60 inches long. The axolotl is a kind of Mexican salamander, unusual because it never loses its gills and can breed without becoming fully adult.

Below: Most amphibians can walk or hop on land, and swim in the water.
Left: Tree frogs, however, live in the trees of tropical rain forests.

common toad

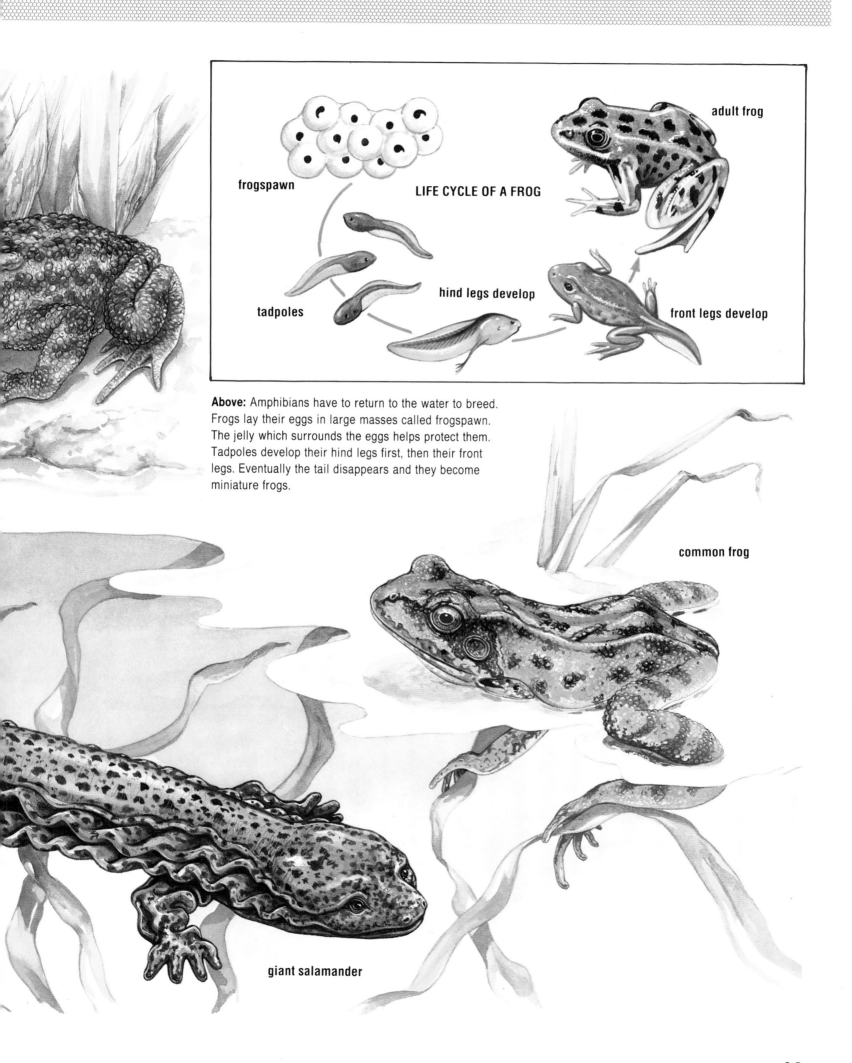

LIFE CYCLE OF A FROG

frogspawn

tadpoles

hind legs develop

front legs develop

adult frog

Above: Amphibians have to return to the water to breed. Frogs lay their eggs in large masses called frogspawn. The jelly which surrounds the eggs helps protect them. Tadpoles develop their hind legs first, then their front legs. Eventually the tail disappears and they become miniature frogs.

common frog

giant salamander

REPTILES

Snakes and lizards are reptiles. They have scaly skins and are cold-blooded creatures. This means that their bodies are not able to keep warm all the time. They need to lie in the sun to warm up, and if they get too hot, they must go into the shade to cool down. Reptiles usually lay eggs but in some species the eggs hatch inside the mother and the young reptiles are born alive.

Most snakes catch and eat other animals for food. Some have hollow fangs which are used to bite their prey. Poisonous venom runs down these teeth from the poison glands. It goes into the body of the victim and kills it. Other snakes, such as pythons, kill their prey by constricting them – the snake coils around the animal and squeezes it until it cannot breathe. Snakes have to swallow their food whole.

The flying snake is one of the few species that climb trees. To move around, it can flatten its body and glide from one tree to another. There are also some snakes that have taken to the water – sea snakes, for example, live far from land.

Crocodiles and alligators are large reptiles which live in lakes and rivers in America, Africa, and Australia. They are meat eaters, living off fish, or animals that come to the water to drink.

Tortoises are also reptiles, with a hard shell which protects their body. They, too, lay eggs and bury them in the ground. Terrapins and turtles spend most of their lives in the water and are good swimmers but have to come ashore onto beaches to lay their eggs in the sand.

giant tortoise

gecko

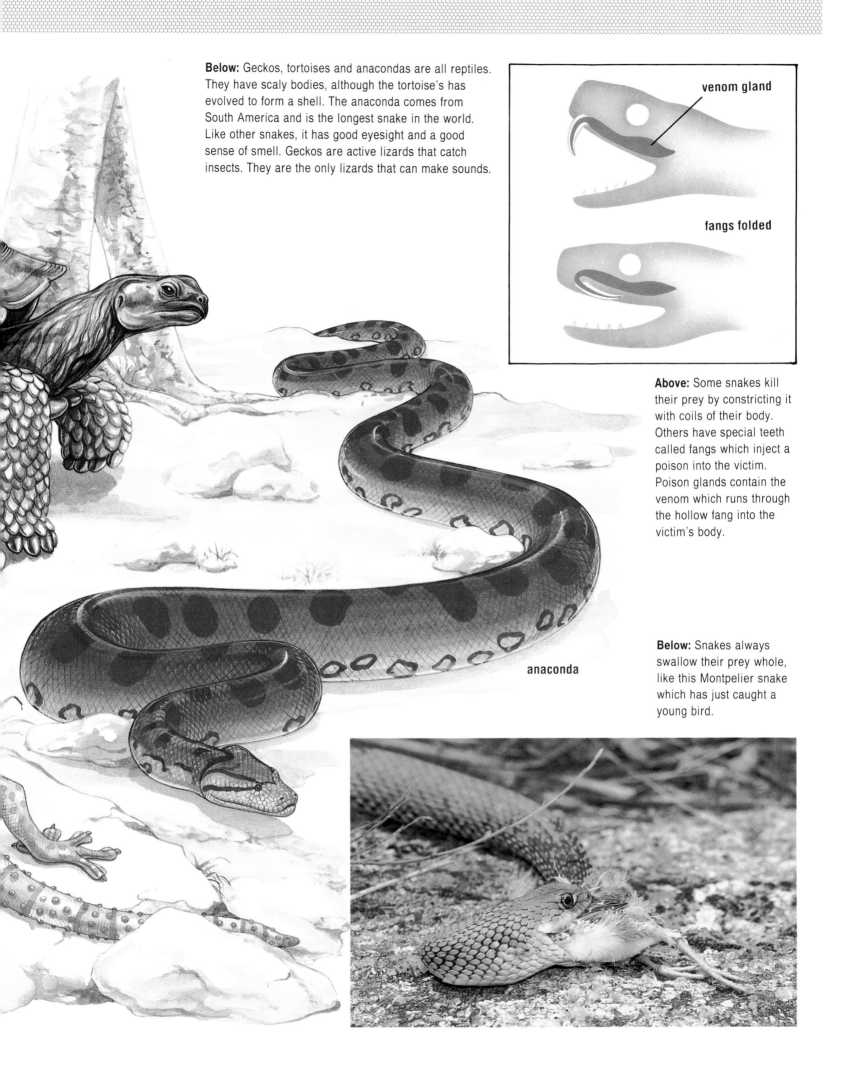

Below: Geckos, tortoises and anacondas are all reptiles. They have scaly bodies, although the tortoise's has evolved to form a shell. The anaconda comes from South America and is the longest snake in the world. Like other snakes, it has good eyesight and a good sense of smell. Geckos are active lizards that catch insects. They are the only lizards that can make sounds.

venom gland

fangs folded

Above: Some snakes kill their prey by constricting it with coils of their body. Others have special teeth called fangs which inject a poison into the victim. Poison glands contain the venom which runs through the hollow fang into the victim's body.

anaconda

Below: Snakes always swallow their prey whole, like this Montpelier snake which has just caught a young bird.

THE WORLD OF BIRDS

1 day   yolk   5 days

baby bird

14 days   wing   21 days ready to hatch

head   eye   leg   leg   eye   beak

Above: Development of a chick inside an egg.

Right: All birds lay eggs and most kinds make a nest in which to incubate them and look after the young after they hatch. Waders such as ringed plovers only make a shallow depression on a beach. Reed warblers weave grasses to make a cup-shaped nest among stems, while skylarks nest on the ground. Magpies make an untidy nest of twigs, and swans lay their eggs on a mound of vegetation.

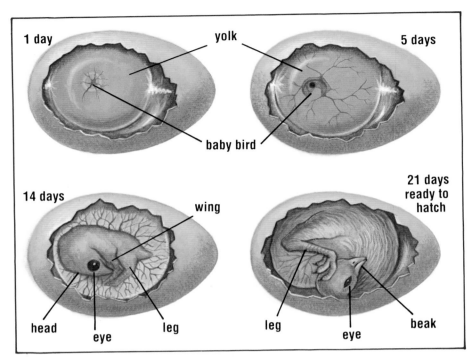

warbler   magpie

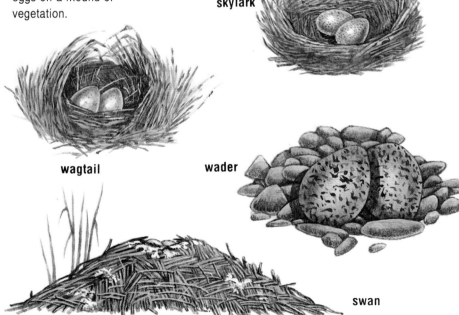

skylark

wagtail   wader

swan

Birds are the only animals that have feathers. They are warm-blooded creatures and their covering of feathers helps keep them warm. The feathers also help birds fly – some keep the bird up in the air, some help control its direction, and others give the bird a smooth shape which makes it easier to move through the air. Feathers are sometimes brightly colored and used to attract a mate. Not all birds fly but they all have wings. They also all have beaks but no teeth.

Young birds develop inside eggs laid by the mother in a nest. In some cases, the parents take it in turns to sit on the eggs and incubate them (keep them warm), or one bird may do it alone.

The food that keeps the baby alive inside the shell is the yellow yolk. At first, the bird is very small indeed and just looks like a small dot. Then its head and body begin to take shape, and when the legs and wings form it begins to look more like a bird. It is constantly growing in size and when it is so big that it fills the shell, it breaks its way out.

Birds are found throughout the world, and over 8,000 species are known. The largest living bird is the ostrich, which cannot fly. It may be up to 8 feet tall. The smallest bird is the bee hummingbird which is only 2 inches long. Its wings beat so fast that they look like a blur.

At the other end of the scale, the albatross seldom beats its enormous wings. It relies on the wind to keep it in the air. Vultures have broad wings which help them to soar high above the ground.

Left: The cuckoo lays its eggs in the nests of other birds, who have to raise the young bird. As soon as it hatches, the cuckoo pushes any other eggs out of the nest.
Below left: Fulmars are related to albatrosses and have long, narrow wings with which they glide over the sea.
Below right: The Californian condor has broad wings for soaring. It is very rare and there are now none living in the wild.

29

ADAPTATIONS IN BIRDS

A bird's beak is a versatile tool. It is used to keep the feathers in good condition, to build nests, and for feeding. Beaks come in all shapes and sizes. Each bird's beak is suited to the food that it eats. Wading birds, such as the dunlin and the godwit, have long, thin beaks which they use to probe the mud. If the beak touches a worm, it pulls it to the surface and the bird eats the worm. The pelican has a large pouch beneath its beak to scoop fish from the water.

Birds that feed on insects often have thin, delicate beaks which are used like tweezers to pick caterpillars and bugs from twigs and leaves. Seed-eating birds have stout, tough beaks which can crush the hard outer casing of the seed. The crossbill is unique because the top half of its bill overlaps the bottom half. This curious shape is just right for extracting seeds from pine cones. Birds of prey and owls have sharp, curved beaks which are used to tear flesh. They also have sharp and powerful talons which grip tightly if the prey is struggling.

The feet of birds are also suited to where they live. Ducks have webbed feet for swimming and woodpeckers have powerful toes and claws for climbing trees.

Nests, too, are very varied. Plovers only make a simple hollow in the ground but weaver birds make complicated nests of woven grass suspended from a branch. Puffins and kingfishers nest in burrows which are dug out with their beaks, while buzzards and storks make nests of twigs in treetops. These big nests may be used year after year by the same birds.

herring gull

common buzzard

carrion crow

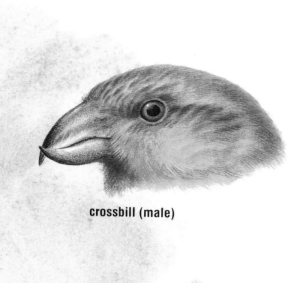

crossbill (male)

common buzzard

common curlew

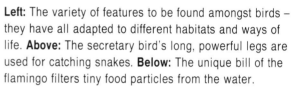

Left: The variety of features to be found amongst birds – they have all adapted to different habitats and ways of life. **Above:** The secretary bird's long, powerful legs are used for catching snakes. **Below:** The unique bill of the flamingo filters tiny food particles from the water.

UNUSUAL BIRDS

Left: Male birds of paradise are among the most beautiful of birds, with their displays of long, colorful plumes. Most of the 42 species live in New Guinea.

Above: Hoatzins are strange-looking birds that live in swamps in South America. They look rather similar to fossil bird ancestors. They feed on leaves and berries, and nest beside rivers. The young have claws on their wings. These help them to climb out of their nest and among the branches when in danger.

Some of the most beautiful birds are the birds of paradise that live in northern Australia and in New Guinea. There are several different kinds but in all cases the males have very lovely feathers which they show when they want to attract a mate.

One of the most primitive birds is the hoatzin which lives by swamps and rivers in South America. If a nest of hoatzins is disturbed, the young climb out among the branches using claws on their wings.

Flamingoes are extraordinary birds with long legs. They wade in deep water and use their strangely

shaped beaks to filter algae from the water. This food contains chemicals which help to give flamingoes their pink color.

Bowerbirds live in the forests of Australia and New Guinea. The brightly colored males make constructions of twigs and branches which they decorate with colored objects. These bowers are designed to attract the drab-colored female.

Arctic terns are migratory birds and they travel the longest distance of any animal on earth. They breed in the Arctic from May until August, then they fly to the Antarctic for the rest of the year. They make this journey every year of their lives.

Penguins live in the seas of the Antarctic. They cannot fly but use their short, powerful wings to swim through the water, fast enough to catch fish. Penguins nest in large colonies on rocky islands. Their dense feathers help keep the birds warm and dry in the cold Antarctic seas, and also keep the eggs warm.

Left: Hummingbirds are the most aerobatic of all birds. Most species live in South America and a few are found in North America. They beat their wings at such a rate that they can hover in one place. They feed on nectar using their long bills and tongues. Some species are small, not much bigger than a bee. Others are as big as a starling and have a large beak.

MAMMALS

Cats, dogs, rabbits, horses, and people are all mammals. Mammals are animals that have warm bodies, with warm blood pumping through them. To help them keep that warmth, mammals are covered with hair or fur. Fur is just soft hair. Some mammals, such as whales and rhinos, do not have much hair but others, such as bears and cats, have thick coats.

Most mammals give birth to live young. A few rather strange mammals still lay eggs, like birds or reptiles do. One of these is the platypus, which lives in and around streams and rivers in Australia. The female lays her eggs in a burrow in the bank.

When the baby platypus hatches, the mother feeds it on her milk. All other mammals also feed their young on milk. It supplies all the goodness the babies need until they are able to feed themselves.

There are more than 4,000 kinds of mammal in the world today, living in a great variety of different environments. Bats have taken to the air and mainly fly at night. Monkeys and squirrels are at home in the trees, while deer, antelope, mice, and voles are found on the ground, grazing on the vegetation. Some mammals, such as moles, can burrow underground, while whales, seals, and dolphins live in the oceans, swimming and diving to great depths.

The smallest mammal in the world is the pygmy shrew which only weighs one-twentieth of an ounce. The largest mammal is the blue whale which may weigh 150 tons. This makes it the largest animal ever to have lived.

Right: Mammals such as this pig give birth to young which are smaller versions of the parents. For their first few months they are fed on milk produced by the mother. This contains all the nutrients they need while they are small.

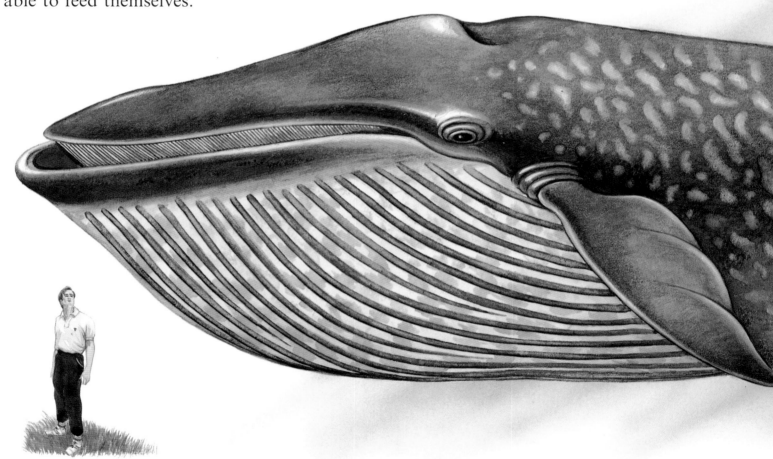

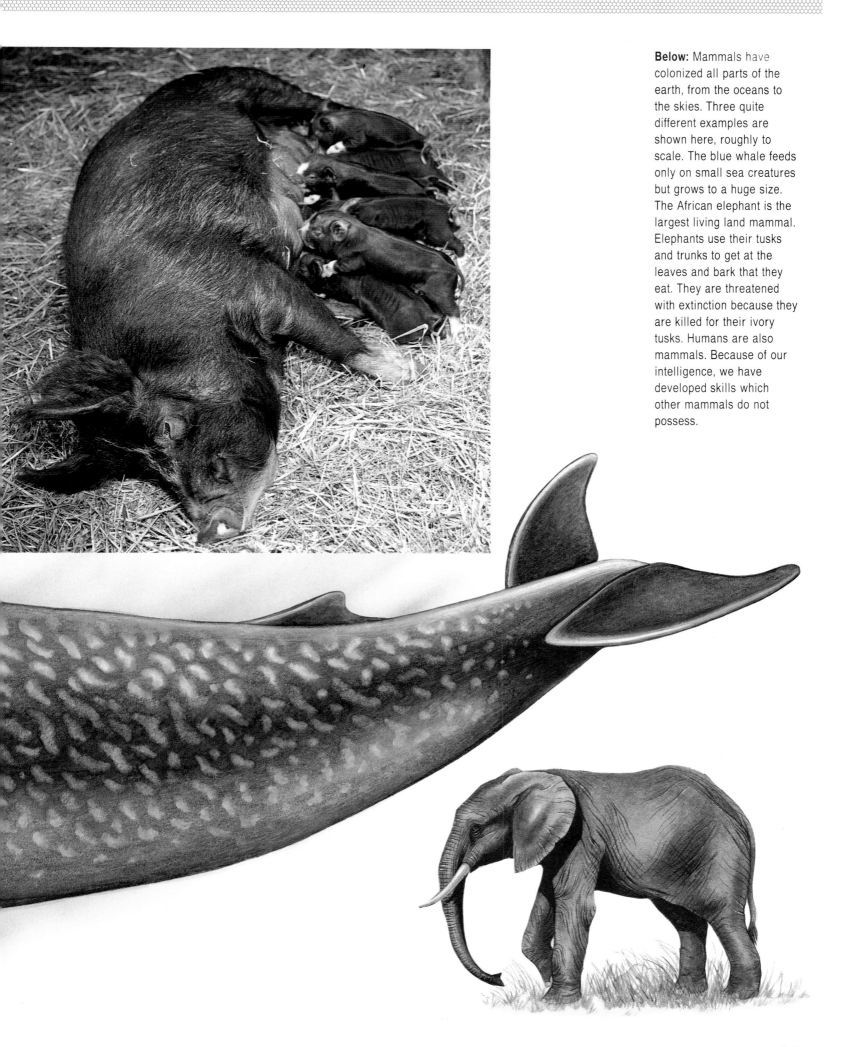

Below: Mammals have colonized all parts of the earth, from the oceans to the skies. Three quite different examples are shown here, roughly to scale. The blue whale feeds only on small sea creatures but grows to a huge size. The African elephant is the largest living land mammal. Elephants use their tusks and trunks to get at the leaves and bark that they eat. They are threatened with extinction because they are killed for their ivory tusks. Humans are also mammals. Because of our intelligence, we have developed skills which other mammals do not possess.

MAMMALS WITH POUCHES

Left: Wallabies are smaller than kangaroos (**right**) but hop in the same way, using their powerful back legs. They eat plants and use their front paws to help them feed. Some kinds of wallabies live in dense forests.
Below: The echidna is a strange looking marsupial covered in spines. Instead of producing live young, the echidna lays an egg. This is kept in its pouch for a few days until it hatches.

Marsupials are mammals that carry their young around in pouches. Most of the marsupials are found in Australia, but a few live in South America. The best known marsupials are kangaroos, but koala bears, possums, wombats, and wallabies are all members of this group.

When they are born, baby marsupials are at a very early stage of their development – they are still blind and naked and very, very small. Baby kangaroos, for example, are about an inch long when they are born, but they are strong enough to crawl up the fur on their mother's stomach and climb into her pouch where they get the milk that they need to continue growing.

The young kangaroo, or joey as it is known, does not venture out of the pouch for the next 33 weeks. It stays inside feeding on its mother's milk. Even after it leaves the pouch, it returns to feed or for protection when threatened.

Right: Koalas are marsupials that live in Australia. They move very slowly and feed on the leaves of eucalyptus, or gum, trees. Koalas are now quite rare, partly because their food plants are being cut down.

When fully grown, red kangaroos stand nearly 6 feet tall. Their powerful hind legs are used for bounding along the ground – at full speed, they can travel at nearly 30 miles per hour, and cover more than 30 feet in a single leap.

Koalas are slow-moving marsupials that live in eucalyptus or gum forests where they eat the leaves and bark of the trees. Female koalas have one young at a time. This is carried around in the pouch and on the mother's back. Sugar gliders are marsupials that look rather like squirrels. They leap from tree to tree using flaps of skin between their front and back legs to help them glide. They may cover up to 300 feet in a single leap. The bushy tail helps them steer.

MAMMALS FROM THE SEA

Whales, dolphins, and seals live in seas and oceans around the world. Although they live under water, they have to come to the surface to breathe air, but only seals and sea lions ever go onto the land.

When whales dive, they hold their breath for up to 40 minutes. On coming to the surface again, they blow out the stale breath, which forms a great spout, and take in fresh air.

The front legs of whales and dolphins have evolved into flippers which, along with their tails, help drive them through the water. Land mammals have fur to keep them warm, but fur would become soaked and cold in the water, so sea mammals have a thick layer of fat, called blubber, to keep them warm.

Right: Dolphins and porpoises are superbly adapted to life in the sea. They are streamlined and have a powerful tail and flippers. Dugongs and manatees are slow moving mammals which feed on underwater plants.

manatee

dolphin

38

Baby whales are fed on their mother's milk, in the same way as other baby mammals. Many kinds of whales and dolphins feed on fish. The larger species of whale often feed on tiny creatures called krill which are very common in the sea. Even though the blue whale eats nothing but krill, it grows to over 100 feet in length.

Seals and walruses can come onto land if they wish, but their bodies do not move as well out of water. The females give birth on land and the young drink their mother's milk there for several days before going into the sea.

Manatees are strange-looking mammals that live in shallow tropical seas. One kind also occurs in the River Amazon. They eat seaweeds and grasses that grow in the water.

Below: Seals come onto land to bask and to give birth to their young. Because their skin is tough, they can move over jagged rocks and boulders.

porpoise

PRIMATES

Monkeys, apes, baboons, and lemurs belong to the same group of animals as humans. We are all called primates.

Monkeys are found in South and Central America, Africa, and Asia. Howler monkeys are found in Central and South America, and have long, powerful tails which are prehensile. This means that they can grip onto things, unlike the tails of most other animals, and are used almost as a fifth limb. Howler monkeys have very loud voices which can carry for considerable distances through the jungle.

Baboons come from Africa and, unlike monkeys, live mainly on the ground. They like to live in large, noisy groups which roam around together in search of food. Members of the group groom each other and warn other baboons of danger with loud screams.

Chimpanzees, gorillas, and orangutans are our nearest relatives. Orangutans come from southeast Asia and are easily recognized by their red, shaggy coats. They have long, powerful arms for climbing trees and their hands and feet have a strong grip.

Gorillas and chimpanzees come from Africa. Chimps live in family groups and roam the forests in search of fruit, nuts, and berries. Gorillas eat shoots and leaves and, although very large, are very gentle animals. Both gorillas and chimps are threatened by hunting and by the destruction of the forests in which they live.

Lemurs live only on the island of Madagascar and most kinds are now rare. The ring-tailed lemur has a tail ringed with black and white which it uses to give signals to other lemurs.

Right: Gorillas live in the forests of West Africa. Some live in the mountains while others live in the lowland forests. Despite their large size, powerful muscles, and fearsome appearance, gorillas are gentle creatures. They live in family groups. Each group has a large, dominant male gorilla as its leader.

Below: Man's nearest relatives, the primates, are found all around the world. Africa has a large number of different kinds. Monkeys, chimps, and gorillas live in the jungles, while baboons live on the open plains. In Asia, monkeys, orangutans, and gibbons can be found.

chimpanzee

gibbon

mandrill

orangutan

baboon

gorilla

spider monkey

lemur

PREDATORY MAMMALS

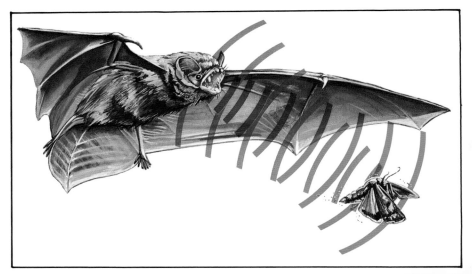

Left: Most kinds of bat can catch moths and other insects in complete darkness. They have their own type of sonar which helps them to locate their prey. They emit a high-pitched noise and listen to the sound as it bounces off the insect's body.

Right: The open plains of East Africa have several different kinds of big cat. Leopards are secretive creatures which stalk their prey on their own. Cheetahs can run at great speeds and catch gazelles and impalas. They have beautiful, spotted coats which give them camouflage. Lions hunt in packs. Each member of the pack cooperates and each shares in the kill.

Below: Otters are good swimmers and can chase and catch fish underwater.

lioness

cheetah

Predators are mammals that have to kill and eat meat to survive. Lions, tigers, wild dogs, otters, and polar bears are all predatory mammals. Some predators only eat meat. Others, such as humans, have a varied diet which includes fruit, seeds, and vegetables.

Lions live in family groups on the plains of Africa. They sometimes hunt as a group and catch animals such as zebras and wildebeest. Female lions and young males do most of the hunting. When the lions have eaten all they want, vultures and hyenas finish off the meal.

Cheetahs, too, live on the grasslands of Africa. They catch gazelles and impalas which they chase at high speed – the cheetah is the fastest land mammal and can run for short distances at an amazing 70 miles per hour.

Tigers inhabit the jungles of India and nearby countries, living on their own rather than in groups. Their stripes make them difficult to see among the branches and fallen leaves and they move quietly through the forest, stalking prey such as deer.

Wolves live in the northern forests of Canada and Russia. In the winter, they live in groups called packs, which sometimes hunt together to catch deer or moose for food. In the summer, wolves feed on fruits, insects, and mice. They are well known for their howls which echo through the forests.

Most kinds of bat are predatory mammals, too. They usually feed on moths, which they catch at night. A few kinds can catch fish or frogs, and vampire bats feed on the blood of other animals.

PLANT-EATING MAMMALS

Animals that eat plants are called herbivores. Many of the mammals we see around us eat plants. Farm animals such as cows, horses, sheep, and goats are herbivores. Deer and rabbits also eat plants and so do elephants and hippopotamuses.

Wildebeest are strange-looking antelope which live on the plains of Africa. They live with zebras in large herds of up to a million animals. Both animals eat grass and have to roam hundreds of miles every year in search of fresh food.

Giraffes are tall herbivores which also live in Africa. Their long necks help them reach the tender shoots and leaves which are out of reach of other animals. They have very tough tongues and lips and can chew even the most spiny of plants.

Herbivores have to eat a lot of leaves and shoots in order to stay alive and it takes a long time for their bodies to extract the nutrients. Cows and sheep have special stomachs which help digestion and which also contain certain bacteria that speed up the process.

Sloths are peculiar mammals that live in the forests of South America. They hang upside down in trees and move very slowly. They feed on leaves and buds which it takes them several days to digest.

Giant pandas live only in China, and are now very rare. They feed on bamboo, spending most of the daylight hours eating the shoots and leaves. Their front paws have a small pad which acts like a thumb to help them grip the bamboo stems while they are eating.

Right: In the fall, the dormouse eats lots of hazelnuts and berries. It stores fat in its body to help it hibernate through the winter. It makes a warm nest of leaves and grasses, and sleeps from October until April. When it wakes up, the dormouse has to eat lots of food to build up its reserves. In spring, it eats oak flowers and catkins.

Left: The giant panda is in danger of extinction due to the destruction of bamboo forests, its main food source.

Below: The wildebeest is a kind of antelope that lives in East Africa. It eats grass and lives in huge herds which migrate long distances to find fresh food.

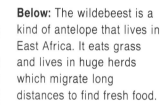

MUSHROOMS AND TOADSTOOLS

If you go into a wood when the weather is damp and warm you may see toadstools growing from the ground. Each one is shaped like a small umbrella. Toadstools are part of a fungus – an unusual form of life which is not an animal and not a plant either. It does not move about like an animal does, and it cannot make its own food as a green plant can. So how does a fungus survive?

The rest of the fungus lies beneath the toadstool, in the soil. From the bottom of the toadstool are many long, white threads which make up the main part of the fungus. These threads make a liquid that can dissolve the little pieces of dead leaves and wood that are in the soil and take back the nutrients into the fungus.

There are many different kinds of fungus (the plural is fungi). Each kind of fungus makes a toadstool of a different shape and color. The toadstool's job is to make spores which grow into new fungus threads. These spores are very tiny so when they fall off they are blown away by the wind and can be spread far and wide. If they land in a suitable place, they will begin to grow.

Some fungi can be eaten – mushrooms, for example, are popular all over the world, and local markets in France and other European countries sell a fascinating variety of edible fungi.

However, you must never eat a fungus that you find growing wild as there are many kinds that are highly poisonous. One of these is called the death cap. It is so poisonous that anyone eating it is almost certain to die.

Right: Puffballs are found among the leaves on the woodland floor in the fall. As the puffball matures, hundreds of thousands of spores form inside and a split opens in the top of the ball. If the puffball is knocked or if a raindrop hits it, the tiny spores are "puffed" out into the air just like talcum powder. All kinds of mushroom and toadstool produce spores. Look underneath a mushroom and you will find gills. These are where the spores are produced. They fall out when they are ripe and are carried away by the wind.

Below: Mushrooms and toadstools come in all shapes and sizes. Some look like balls, and others like little bonnets. Many kinds, such as the field mushroom and penny bun, are good to eat, but others are highly poisonous.

amethyst agaric

chanterelle

inkcap

moss pixy cap

boletus

death cap

earth ball

cup fungus

Above: When food is left too long, mold grows on it. One kind of mold is called penicillin. This produces chemicals that we use as medicines.

fly agaric

morel

fairy ring toadstool

puff ball

helmet cap   sulphur tuft   purple stereum

THE WORLD OF PLANTS

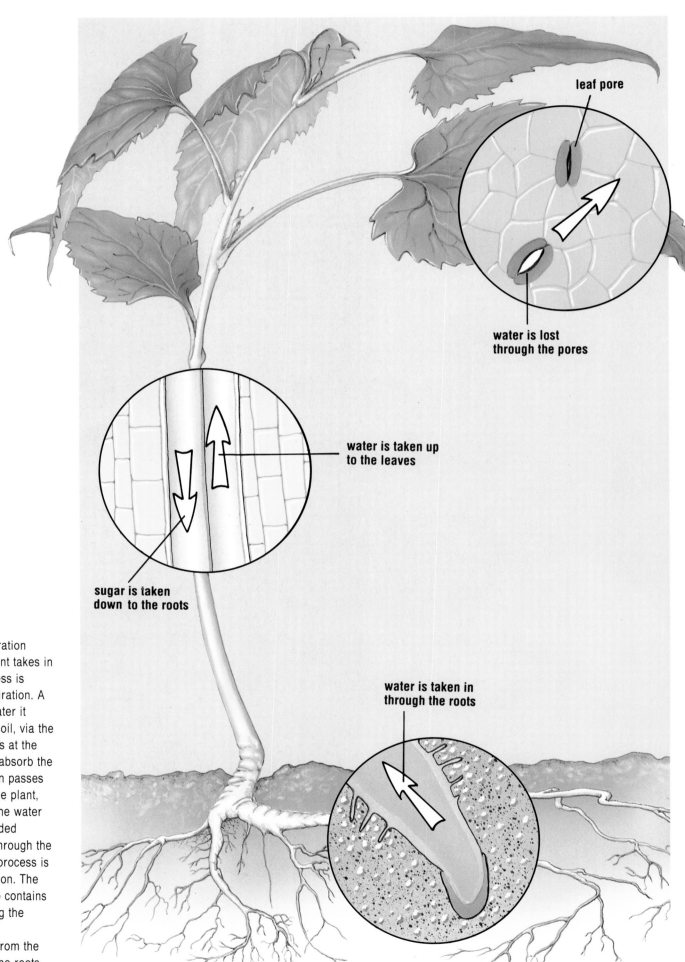

leaf pore

water is lost
through the pores

water is taken up
to the leaves

sugar is taken
down to the roots

water is taken in
through the roots

Right: This illustration shows how a plant takes in water. The process is known as transpiration. A plant gets the water it needs from the soil, via the roots. Small hairs at the end of the roots absorb the water, which then passes up the stem of the plant, through tubes. The water which is not needed evaporates out through the leaf pores. This process is called transpiration. The plant's stem also contains tubes for carrying the sugars, made by photosynthesis, from the leaves down to the roots.

What is the difference between an animal and a plant? Both live, feed, and reproduce but it is how they do this that varies. Plants cannot move in the same way as animals can. This means that they have to get their food in one place. They do this by using their roots and their green leaves, through a process called photosynthesis.

During the daytime, the leaves make food for the plant. They use water that comes up from the soil, together with a part of the air called carbon dioxide, which is taken into the plant through tiny pores in the surface of the leaf. With the help of energy trapped by the leaves from sunlight, the plant uses the water and carbon dioxide to make a kind of sugar. This is the basic food for plants.

After the sugar has been made, the plant gives off another gas – oxygen. Both plants and animals need oxygen in order to breathe, so without plants, no form of life could survive.

Plants have a network of roots under the ground. These help to anchor the plant in the ground but they are also used for taking up water, salt, and nutrients from the soil. These all pass through tubes from the roots, up the stem and to the leaves. Other tubes carry the sugars from the leaves to the roots.

Some plants are very small and simple, such as mosses and liverworts, while flowering plants can often grow to a great size. The coastal redwood trees of California are the largest plants in the world.

Right: The famous giant redwood, also known as the giant sequoia, is a conifer that grows to over 250 feet in height. The tallest in the world is 270 feet tall, with a circumference of more than 78 feet.

PLANTS WITHOUT FLOWERS

Mosses can often be seen in woods, making soft, green cushions on the ground. But they also grow on old walls and roofs, where it is much drier. Mosses never have flowers or make seeds so they have to reproduce in other ways. Often, pieces are broken off and moved away, perhaps by the wind or rain, or animals brushing against them. If they end up in a suitable place, they will begin to grow again. This is one way mosses reproduce.

At certain times of the year, very thin stalks may grow up from some moss plants. At the end of the stalks are tiny spore boxes. When the spores are ripe, a little lid falls off and the spores come out. They are so light that every puff of wind blows them away. When they land, they can begin to grow into new moss plants.

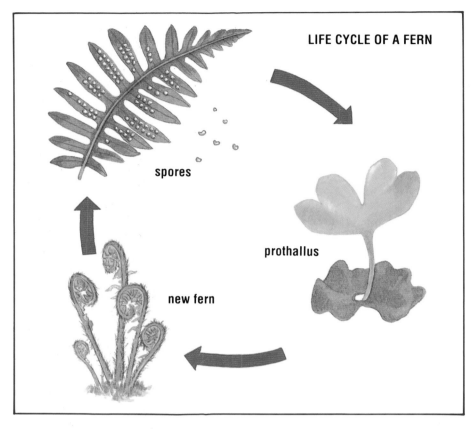

LIFE CYCLE OF A FERN

spores

prothallus

new fern

Above: Each spore grows into a tiny prothallus. This produces male and female cells which then combine to form an adult fern.

Below: Ferns like to grow where the soil and air are damp. You can find them on shady walls, on riverbanks, and in wet woodland.

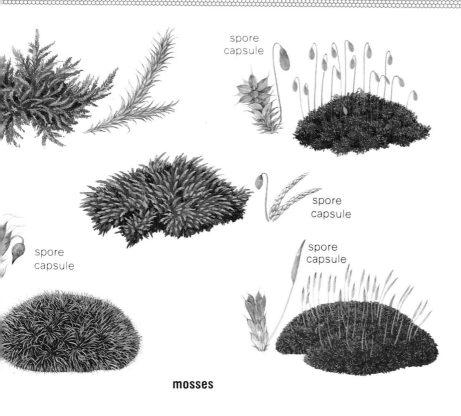

spore
capsule

spore
capsule

spore
capsule

spore
capsule

mosses

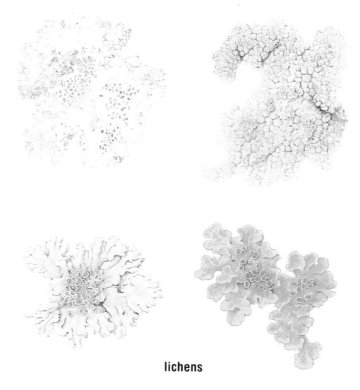

lichens

Above: Mosses and liverworts are primitive plants that grow very slowly. Some mosses are feathery while others grow in neat little "cushions". Lichens do not like pollution so very few kinds are found in large towns. Many more types occur by the sea.

Liverworts are also plants that have no flowers. They grow very slowly and like damp and shady places. They are often found on riverbanks or on rock faces dripping with water.

Ferns reproduce by spores, too. They usually lie in special places on the undersides of the leaves. When it first lands, a spore grows into a small heart-shaped plant before eventually growing into a large fern.

Ferns are taller than mosses and have larger leaves, called fronds. Some have leaves like straps, some are like huge feathers. There are tree ferns that grow in tropical countries more than 13 feet tall. There have been ferns on earth for many, many years. The coal that is dug out of the ground today was formed from ferns and other plants that grew in marshy places millions of years ago.

51

PLANT REPRODUCTION

For flowering plants to reproduce, the female part usually has to be fertilized by the male part of another plant. In flowering plants the male part is called the pollen and the female is the ovary.

Plants have developed lots of ways of getting the pollen to the ovary. In grasses and many trees, the wind distributes the pollen, which is like yellow dust. Most plants that have brightly colored petals depend on insects for pollination. The insects are attracted to a flower by the color and the sweet nectar in it. The insect, such as a bee, crawls into the flower to collect the nectar and the pollen rubs off onto its body. It then flies to another flower and the pollen rubs off onto the ovary.

Right: Flowers contain the reproductive parts of the plant. The male parts – the pollen – are carried on the tips of the anthers. The female parts of the flower, called the ovaries, are in the middle of the flower.

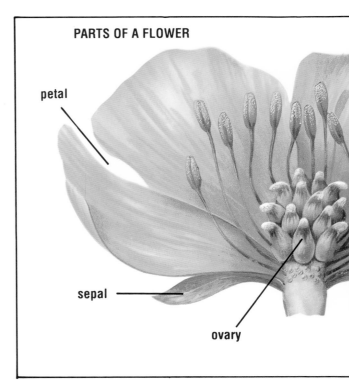

PARTS OF A FLOWER

petal

sepal

ovary

sycamore

grasses

dandelion

burr

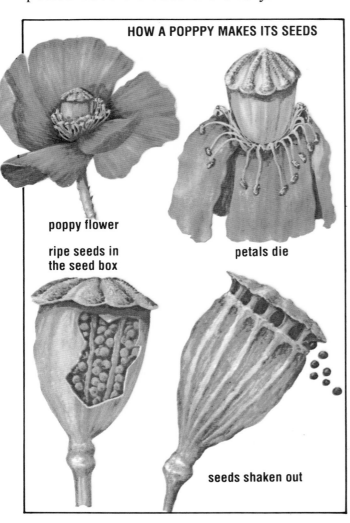

HOW A POPPPY MAKES ITS SEEDS

poppy flower

petals die

ripe seeds in the seed box

seeds shaken out

anther

stamen

ovule

Below center: In order to produce new generations of plants, the pollen of one flower must fertilize the ovary of another. Some flowers use insects, such as bees, to carry the pollen for them. Their flowers are colorful so that the bees are attracted to them. The pollen of other plants, such as grasses, is very small and light. It is carried from one plant to another by the wind.

Then a very strange thing happens. A very small tube begins to grow from each pollen grain. It grows through the ovary wall until it reaches an ovule. The contents of the pollen grain move down the tube and join the contents of the ovule. The ovule has now been fertilized. The ovule then grows to become a seed, which will later grow into a new plant.

There are many different kinds of seed and many different ways of making them spread as far away as possible. Dandelion seeds are blown by the wind, poppy seeds are shaken out of their seed box like pepper from a pepper-shaker, and burdock seeds stick to the fur of animals. Some seeds, such as sycamore, have "wings" which keep them in the air. Seeds are often encased in berries which are eaten by birds or other small animals. The seeds inside pass through the gut unharmed and are later deposited far away.

foxglove

Below: When a flower is fertilized it forms a seed. Plants try to spread their seeds as far as possible. Berries are often eaten by birds and carried long distances until they are passed with the droppings. Other seeds, such as the sycamore's, have "wings" which carry them far away. Coconut seeds can float and are carried by the sea.

UNUSUAL PLANTS

There are at least 250,000 kinds of flowering plant. The plants and their flowers come in all shapes and sizes. The flower of duckweed, which floats on ponds, is so small that it is hard to see. But the flower of a plant called rafflesia, which grows in the jungles of Asia, may measure as much as 3 feet across.

Plants grow in all kinds of places. Cacti are plants that can grow in very dry places, such as deserts. When it does rain, they store water in their stems, to be used whenever they need it. Their flowers are very lovely but very rare – some kinds of cacti do not flower very often.

Most plants have green leaves which help them make their food. A few kinds of plant do not make their own food but instead eat decaying matter. They are called saprophytes. The bird's-nest orchid, for example, lives in the deep shade of beechwoods and feeds on rotten leaves.

Some plants feed on other living plants. They are called parasites. Mistletoe attacks apple trees and feeds on their sap. There are even a few carnivorous plants. Certain leaves on pitcher plants are shaped like pots and have water in the bottom. Sometimes an insect will land on the rim of the pot, slip and fall into the pitcher, where it stays until it dies and rots. The plant produces a liquid that helps dissolve the soft parts of the insect, releasing nutrients that the plant can use for food.

Sundew also traps insects on its sticky leaves, and the Venus's fly-trap has leaves which close around any prey that lands on them.

Top left: Some plants live to a great age. Bristlecone pines grow in the White Mountains of California. Many of the trees are more than a thousand years old and are the oldest living things in the world. **Bottom left:** The cuckoo pint attracts small flies to its strange flower. Trapped inside, the flies become covered in pollen. Eventually they escape and take the pollen to the flower of another cuckoo pint. **Right:** Three carnivorous plants, which catch and feed on insects.

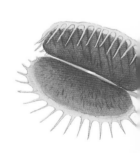

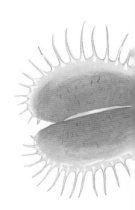

pitcher plant

sundew

Venus's fly-trap

LIFE AT THE POLES

At the far north and the far south of the Earth are the poles. These are both very cold regions with ice and snow everywhere. The northern polar region is called the Arctic and the southern polar region is called the Antarctic.

When spring comes to the Arctic, the snow begins to melt. Herds of reindeer feed on the mosses, lichens, and small plants that appear from underneath the snow. Lemmings, which are small rodents, also eat these plants but they, in turn, are eaten by arctic foxes and long-tailed skuas (like a gull). Snowy owls are also found in the Arctic. They are large, white birds which prey on lemmings and arctic hares.

Polar bears live among the pack ice of the Arctic. They have a thick coat which keeps them warm throughout the year, even when they are swimming in the cold sea, catching the seals and fish that they live on. Polar bears are the largest land predator on earth.

The Antarctic does not have as many kinds of wildlife as the Arctic, although it does have several types of penguin. Penguins eat fish and, although they cannot fly, they are strong swimmers – their wings have evolved into flippers. The largest kind is the emperor penguin which nests in large colonies many miles from the sea. Their main enemy is the leopard seal which can swim and catch them underwater. The feathers of penguins are especially adapted to keep them warm and dry when swimming in the cold sea.

1 longtailed skua	9 elephant seal
2 reindeer	10 polar bear
3 snowy owl	11 crab-eating seal
4 arctic fox	12 emperor penguin
5 arctic hare	13 lemming
6 wolves	14 polar cod
7 elk	15 leopard seal
8 common seal	16 adelie penguin

LIFE IN THE DESERTS

Deserts are places where there is very little rain. Hot deserts are found in America, Africa, and Australia. Some deserts are sandy and others are rocky. It is not easy for plants to grow in these hot deserts, but some, such as cacti, can survive because they store water when it rains. Cacti grow only in American deserts. The largest are the saguaros which grow like huge candlesticks and are over 50 feet high.

When the rains come, many desert plants suddenly grow from seeds buried in the sand. They flower, make their seeds, and then die. The Mojave Desert in California and the Negev desert in Israel are two of the places where this happens.

A few animals are able to live in deserts. The kangaroo rats of North American deserts and the jerboas of North Africa survive on seeds, and since these seeds also contain moisture they do not need to find water to drink. They stay underground during the day, coming out at night when it is cooler.

As in other environments, where there are plant-eaters, there will be meat-eaters as well. Fennec foxes, for example, live in Africa, and coyotes and rattlesnakes live in America.

Camels are able to live in very dry places because they can go for a long time without water. But they do not store it; their humps are, in fact, made of fat and it is this that supplies their food needs.

1 red kangaroo
2 bearded dragon
3 Arabian camel
4 fennec fox
5 rattlesnake
6 elf owl

LIFE ON THE SAVANNA

The savanna is a vast area of grassland and scattered thorn trees in parts of Africa, home to millions of grazing animals such as wildebeest, zebra, and topi. These animals wander the grassland in search of food and often have to walk for hundreds of miles before they find an area where rain has fallen.

Although grass dominates the landscape, a few trees and bushes can also be seen. Acacias are flat-topped trees that have spiny twigs and leaflets. These discourage grazing animals but giraffes have tough tongues and lips so they can eat the foliage.

Elephants and rhinoceroses also live on the African savannas. Rhinos graze grass, while elephants often eat the leaves from bushes and trees. Both are threatened by poachers who kill the elephants for their tusks and the rhinos for their horns.

There are lots of meat-eating animals on the African plains. Cheetahs chase impalas, lions attack zebras and wildebeest, and leopards catch antelopes. Vultures, hyenas, and jackals eat any meat that the cats leave.

There are large areas of grassland in other countries too, all with their own kinds of animals. In North America, the prairies were once home to millions of bison. In the South American pampas, there are flightless birds called rheas. In the USSR, the steppes are home to a large bird called the great bustard.

1 elephant
2 cheetah
3 springbok
4 wildebeest
5 ostrich
6 rhinoceros
7 giraffe
8 zebra
9 vervet monkey
10 lion

LIFE IN THE RAIN FORESTS

In parts of South America, Africa, Australia, and southeast Asia, it is very hot and humid, with a lot of rain. Plants here grow very quickly. Trees grow very tall and close together and they have long creepers hanging down from them. These areas of jungle are called rain forests.

Many of the trees are very tall and so close together that their branches and leaves stop much of the sunlight reaching the ground. This makes it hard for small plants to grow. If you fly over a rain forest, it is so dense it looks like a thick, green carpet.

Among the trees and plants live many kinds of animals, although most of them are quite shy and stay well hidden. Birds can be heard up in the treetops but they are difficult to see. Monkeys and gibbons live up there, too, high in the branches. At night, hunting mammals, such as the jaguars and ocelots of South America roam the forest. There are also bright grasshoppers, big butterflies and, on the forest floor, many beetles, snakes, lizards, and frogs.

1 scarlet macaw
2 toucan
3 poison dart frog
4 jackson chameleon
5 cayman
6 orangutan
7 hummingbird

LIFE IN WOODLANDS

In much of the world it is not too hot in the summer nor too cold in the winter. A large part of North America is like this, and much of Europe, too. In these areas you will find small woods and large forests of trees such as oak, beech, maple, and silver birch. Beneath the tall trees grow shorter shrubs. Even smaller than these are the herbs – any plant that does not have a woody stem, such as bluebells and nettles.

These woods and forests grow where there are four seasons in the year: spring, summer, fall, and winter. In winter, almost everything looks dead. But as spring comes, buds begin to form. The small plants must flower and make seeds before the trees get their leaves and shut out the light from the sun.

By late spring and summer, there is plenty of food for plant-eaters such as squirrels, mice, and voles. There are also plenty of insects for the birds which are busy at this time building nests to lay their eggs in.

When fall comes, the leaves begin to change color, becoming beautiful shades of orange, brown, yellow, and red, before dropping from the trees.

When the weather starts to grow colder, some animals store food for the coming winter. Many birds fly south to escape the cold weather.

1 gray squirrel
2 marsh tit
3 woodcock
4 black bear
5 rabbit
6 common frog
7 fox
8 stag
9 polecat
10 woodmouse
11 white-lipped banded snail

LIFE ON THE SEASHORE

Lots of plants and animals live on the seashore. Twice each day the level of the sea moves up the beach and back down again, covering and uncovering these creatures. This regular movement of the sea is called the tide.

All sorts of seaweeds are found on the seashore. Long, strap-like seaweeds, called kelp, grow low down on the shore and are covered in water most of the time. Smaller kinds, called wracks, grow higher up the shore where the sea reaches less often.

Rockpools are often found along the seashore. As the tide drops, animals get left behind in the pools, so it is easy for us to see them. Little fish called blennies and gobies hide in rock crevices. Crabs live under stones and seaweed, while limpets and anemones stick tight to the rocks. Starfish and urchins are sometimes found in these pools also.

On sandy or muddy beaches, you will find ragworms and lugworms living in burrows. Razorshells and cockles also dig in the mud to keep hidden from predators such as birds.

The highest point that the sea reaches each day is called the high-tide line. Above this is the splash zone where spray from the waves reaches. Orange-colored lichens and plants such as thrift grow here.

Seabirds breed on the sides of cliffs above the seashore. Gulls, guillemots, and razorbills nest on ledges and among the boulders. Puffins dig burrows in the soft soil.

1 serrated wrack
2 shanny
3 anemone
4 common starfish
5 sea urchin
6 mussel
7 rock goby
8 hermit crab
9 bladder wrack
10 shore crab
11 sea holly
12 orange lichen
13 sea kale
14 sea campion
15 rock samphire
16 puffin
17 black-headed gull
18 gull

LIFE IN THE OCEANS

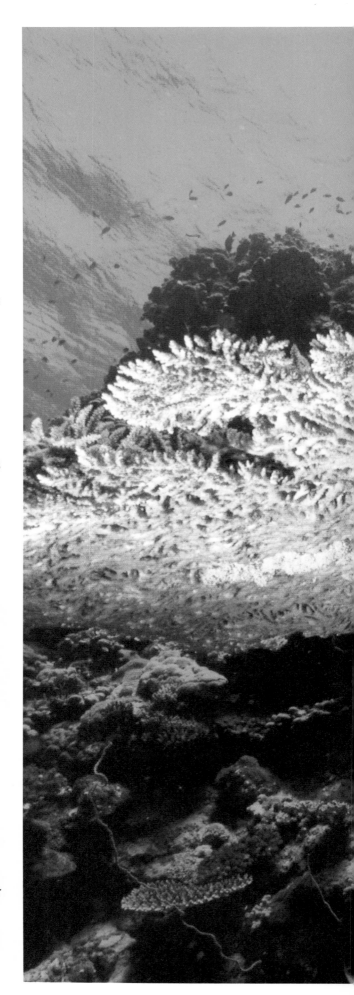

There are millions of plants and animals living in the sea. Most of the plants living in the oceans are extremely small and float near the surface of the water in their thousands. They are food for huge numbers of small animals that also live near the surface. Together, they are all known as plankton.

Many fish feed on this plankton, including one of the largest – the whale shark. Despite their great size, certain whales, too, live entirely on plankton.

The blue whale is the largest animal ever to live. It grows to a length of over 100 feet. The humpback whale is a smaller kind and has long flippers. It can jump right out of the water. The Californian gray whale makes long migrations every year – it spends the summer feeding in the Arctic but swims south to the warmer waters off the coast of Mexico in the winter. The females give birth in the shallow, warm water there.

Many of the fish in the sea may be eaten by other meat-eaters – sharks, for example, are some of the fastest hunters, although not all of them eat other fish.

Deep down in the oceans live many strange fish. It is so dark down there that many of these fishes have "lights" on them, which are used for attracting smaller fish for the larger ones to eat.

Jellyfish are peculiar-looking creatures ranging in size from a fraction of an inch to 6 feet across. They don't really swim but drift in the currents of the open oceans. Although they contain a powerful sting, they are often eaten by turtles. Turtles are reptiles that spend most of their lives at sea, only coming ashore to lay their eggs on sandy beaches.

Right: Coral reefs are found in tropical oceans around the world. The Great Barrier Reef of Australia is the largest but there are other reefs surrounding many tropical islands. Corals are small animals, related to jellyfish. Each one produces a hard casing and together these gradually build up to form a reef. Coral reefs are home to thousands of other animals. Colorful fish, starfish, and anemones all live there. Some of the fish swim in shoals. Others live on their own and shelter in crevices and caves amongst the coral.

LIFE IN RIVERS AND LAKES

onds, rivers, lakes, and canals have lots of plants and animals living both in the fresh water and along the banks.

Willow trees and colorful flowers such as yellow flag iris, water forget-me-not and purple loosestrife all grow along the water's edge so they can keep their roots in water. Water lilies prefer the open water. They have long roots which reach down to the mud at the bottom. The tiny leaves of duckweed, on the other hand, have short roots which float on the surface.

The water is home to a great many fish. Minnows live in groups called shoals, while sticklebacks prefer to live on their own. In the breeding season, the males change color and become red and blue, to attract the female sticklebacks. The female lays her eggs in a little nest the male has built – it is also the male who guards the eggs and young.

There are lots of insects living in the water and among the waterside plants. Water beetles, for example, are often seen swimming across the surface. Dragonfly larvae live on the stream bed until spring, when the adult insect emerges from the water. Mayflies all hatch at the same time and fly off in great swarms.

Many birds live close to water – coots, moorhens, grebes, and ducks are the most common. Herons are quite large water birds with long legs and necks. Their pointed beaks are ideal for catching fish. Water voles are shy creatures that live along the water's edge.

1 heron
2 dragonfly
3 water shrew
4 whirligig beetle
5 perch
6 pike
7 female common mallard

LIFE IN TOWNS AND CITIES

In Europe and North America, there are lots of large towns and cities and the parks and gardens in these towns are important places for wildlife. Most of the flowers in gardens are grown especially for their colors and shapes. Since insects such as bees and butterflies also like such flowers, they come to feed on the nectar and pollen.

There are some insects found in gardens which are not welcomed by gardeners. Aphids or plant lice feed on the sap of roses and vegetable plants and can make the plant wilt. Ladybugs, however, eat hundreds of aphids and are seen as a gardener's friend.

Birds visit our gardens to feed and nest. Blackbirds, robins, sparrows, finches, and thrushes are present all year round. Swallows and martins visit in the summer, and in winter, starlings and tits come to feed.

Mammals also come to the garden, although they often visit at night. In Britain, foxes and hedgehogs are sometimes found living in the middle of cities. In

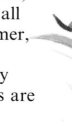

North America; opossums and raccoons are often seen.
Wasteland is soon colonized by colorful flowers such
as ragwort. Freeway right-of-ways and railroad cuts
are also important places for plants because, although
noisy, they are never disturbed by humans. The grassy
strips are home to mice and voles. These small animals
are prey to the kestrels who hover overhead.

1 kestrel	10 ladybug
2 swallow	11 robin
3 gray squirrel	12 tortoise-shell butterfly
4 hedgehog	13 mouse
5 badger	14 badger
6 fox	15 burnet moth
7 rabbit	16 thrush
8 blue tit	17 starling
9 bee	18 blackbird

MAN AND NATURE

Left: Bees are colonial insects that live in hives. Within a colony there is only one queen but there are thousands of other bees. Their job is to collect pollen and nectar, guard the hive, and look after the young bees.

Plants are important to us. Think of all the plants we eat. There are potatoes and beans, tomatoes and onions, apples and cherries, and many others.

Plants such as wheat and rice are eaten everywhere. Wheat can be ground into flour for making bread and cakes. In countries in the East, rice is more important than wheat and is eaten at every meal.

Some plants give us clothing. Many clothes are made from cotton, which grows on small bushes. Trees are used to make wood for furniture and paper for books. Other plants are used to make medicines.

Many animals, such as cows, pigs, and sheep, are reared on farms to provide us with food, but they have other uses as well. Cows and horses are used to pull heavy loads and in the past have even carried soldiers into battle. Dairy cows give us milk which we drink or make into butter, cheese, or yogurt.

Sheep are kept in some parts of America for their meat and wool, but much bigger herds are kept by sheep farmers in Australia and New Zealand.

Even some insects are useful to us. Bees produce honey, and silk moth caterpillars spin silk which is then made into fabric.

1 sheep
2 poultry chicken
3 Fresian cow
4 pig
5 Charolais cow
6 goose
7 duck

CONSERVATION

Many of our industries produce chemicals which harm the plants and animals in the environment. This is called pollution. Big factories and power stations produce pollution but they are encouraged to keep the amount they produce as small as possible. Even automobiles produce polluting gases in the exhaust fumes.

Many ponds, marshes, forests, and heathlands are threatened by development. Sometimes people want to build houses or roads or turn the land into farmland. Other people try to protect some of these habitats by making nature reserves. They also make sure the rarest animals and plants are not in danger of dying out. This is called conservation.

Sometimes conservation is too late and a plant or animal may die out forever. This is called extinction. The dodo was a large flightless bird that once lived on the island of Mauritius. It did not need to fly because nothing attacked it. When man discovered Mauritius, however, he found the dodos all too easy to catch and had soon killed them all. The North American passenger pigeons were all shot by the beginning of this century. Once there were countless millions of them, now there are none left.

Today, many people are trying to save the rain forests before it is too late. Rain forests are found in hot, steamy regions of Africa, South America, and Asia. The best known area is the Amazon in Brazil. If the forests are all cut down, scientists think it will have such an effect on the atmosphere that the whole climate of the earth will be changed.

Left: Pollution and conservation (**below**) are important to all of us. Without a healthy environment, many plants and animals would soon die out. **Right:** The dodo became extinct by the end of the 17th century, killed by sailors for food.

INDEX

ACKNOWLEDGMENTS

PHOTOGRAPHS

All photographs courtesy of Nature Photographers Ltd
S.C. Bisserot 8 top, 20; Brinsley Burbidge 47 right, 54 top, 54 bottom; N.A. Callow 13 bottom; Kevin Carlson 27; Colin Carver 36; R.S. Daniell 33, 45; E.A. Janes 34, 45 top; J.F. Reynolds 31; Don Smith 21, 68/69; Paul Sterry 8 bottom, 11, 13 top, 14, 15, 24, 47 left;
with the exception of the following pages
Mary Evans Picture Library 77
Vicky Hanson 47
Frank Lane Picture Agency 41
Oxford Scientific Films 74

ILLUSTRATIONS

Linden Artists/Mick Loates 10/11, 18/19, 22/23, 30/31, 38/39; Jane Pickering 50, 52/53, 55; Phil Wier 24/25, 26/27, 70/71;
Maltings Partnership 6/7, 28 top, 34/35;
John Martin Artists/Steve Holden 4/5, 58/59, 60/61, 62/63, 64/65, 72/73, 74/75, 76/77;
Oxford Illustrators 12/13, 16/17, 34/35, 36/37, 42/43, 44/45;
Bernard Thornton Artists/Fred Anderson 56/57, 66/67.

Other illustrations © The Octopus Publishing Group Limited